Servings with Love

Entertaining Ways for Special Days

by Elizabeth Pistole
with daughters
Cynthia Poikonen and Carole Bagwell

ISBN 0-87162-245-9

Table of Contents

The Joy of . . .

The joy of entertaining in your own way is the theme for these new volumes of *Servings with Love*. Again it has been a most enjoyable task to work with the entire family as Cindy, Carole, and I endeavored to plan menus, share the recipes, and talk about the joy of many things. We have moved recently from the home we lived in for almost twenty-three years, and the main joy in the new home is our dining room. Our meals were served in the family room at the other home, but it surely is easier now not to have to put the drop leaf dining table down quickly so that the gang can watch football or basketball or baseball or whatever.

My greatest appreciation is given to my husband, Hollis, who stands by with a ready hand in all of the entertaining endeavors. He is the greatest. Our son David is busy working on his doctorate, so his culinary experiments have temporarily halted, but it is good to see him enjoy a "home-cooked" meal when he is able to get home. Our youngest son, John, is finishing his work at law school and is now married to lovely Kathy Harp. We love having her in our family, and she shares often of her culinary skills in making breads, creating delightful desserts, or preparing unusual salads.

My deep appreciation also goes to wonderful friends who have generously shared their recipes. I am grateful.

—Elizabeth

I love to cook and I enjoy trying different recipes. It has been fun and rewarding to cook for my husband, Carl, and our three-year-old son, Stephen. One evening after a meal we all seemed to enjoy, Stephen looked at me and said, "You're a good cook, mama." That certainly makes it all worthwhile.

I have worn many hats as a daughter, sister, friend, student, and teacher, but there is, for me, nothing as rewarding as being a wife and mother. Cooking has involved a large part of my time as a homemaker, and I know that for the next few years it will continue. To know that my husband and son are appreciative helps to offset those days when I simply don't feel like cooking.

Carl is of Finnish descent and it has been interesting to try recipes that are favorites from Finland. We may not always like them, but it has been a tasty challenge. He has been patient when he comes home and finds the counters covered with food, and as he starts to sample an item I warn, "Don't eat that, it's for the bazaar and bake sale!" Thanks, Carl, you are special.

—Cindy

It's so much fun and so rewarding to cook for people who appreciate my efforts. My husband, Tim, probably doesn't have the interest that I do in food, but he's very aware of what I serve. And his comments about what I fix are always appreciated—well, almost always! Even more important, though, is his willingness at least to try whatever I've made. From Matador's Mania to Sweet Licorice Treat, he's right there to taste it—if only once. And I love him for it!

Our three-year-old son, Todd, isn't as charitable as his father with regards to trying unusual foods. But I like his honesty about what he does eat, even when it's not always what I want to hear. Leave it to him to announce to everyone at the table that the gravy is "very lumpy tonight"!

It's too early to tell how our eight-month-old son, Mark, is going to respond to my adventures in cooking, but I have a suspicion he's going to approach food with a real gusto and excitement. He'll fit right in with the rest of us then!

—Carole

Apple Festival Party

Menu

(Serves 6)

Apple Cider Punch

Apple Smothered Pork Chops

Yam and Apple Casserole

Apple Stuffed Acorn Squash

Beet Apple Salad

Apple Coleslaw

Autumn Apple Bread

Apple Pandowdy   **Fresh Apple Cake**

When we kept our three-year-old grandson, Todd, the other day we taught him the old adage, "an apple a day keeps the doctor away." Immediately his imaginative mind gleefully added another verse, "and a banana a day keeps the nurse away."

As we thought about the apple we took one from the fruit bowl and talked about it. We felt it, smelled the delicious aroma and I showed him how my father could start at the top of the apple and peel it around and around without ever breaking the peeling. It was such fun.

How long has it been since you looked—really looked—at a ripe apple just plucked from the tree? Wonder and appreciation are heightened through our senses as we pause and savor with all our senses. We "experience" the apple as a "thing of beauty and a joy forever."

—Elizabeth

Apple Cider Punch

1 quart apple cider
1 quart tea (instant with lemon),
   mixed
1 quart orange juice
1 8- or 9-ounce package cinnamon
   red hots

*Heat all together and serve as guests
arrive.*

Apple Smothered Pork Chops

6 center-cut lean pork chops
¾ t. salt
¼ t. ground sage
3 tart apples
3 T. molasses
3 T. flour
2 cups hot water
1 T. cider vinegar
⅓ cup yellow raisins

*Sprinkle pork chops with ¼ t. salt and
¼ t. sage. Brown chops slowly in hot
skillet. Reserve fat drippings in skillet.
Put chops in large shallow baking dish.
Peel and core apples and cut across
in ¼-inch slices; arrange on chops.
Pour molasses over top. Stir flour into
fat in skillet; cook until brown, stirring
while it cooks. Gradually stir in water
and cook until mixture boils. Add
vinegar, ½ t. salt, and raisins. Pour
sauce over chops and apples. Cover
and bake in preheated oven 350° for
about 1 hour.*

Yam and Apple Casserole
Serves 10 to 12

4 large yams
3 large cooking apples
3 T. butter or margarine
1 T. cornstarch
½ cup firmly packed brown sugar
1 T. fresh lemon juice
2 cups apple juice, hot
½ ground allspice
½ ground cinnamon
⅓ cup raisins

Boil the yams until tender; peel and slice ⅓ inch thick. Peel, core, and thinly slice apples. Melt butter or margarine; add cornstarch and sugar. Mix in lemon juice, hot apple juice, and spices. Continue to cook for 5 or 6 minutes. In shallow greased casserole dish, alternate layers of sliced yams and apples. Sprinkle raisins over top. Pour the hot apple juice mixture over ingredients, cover with foil, and bake for 1 hour in 375° oven. Remove foil and continue baking for another 30 minutes, basting frequently.

Apple Stuffed Acorn Squash
Serves 6.

3 acorn squash
3 tart red apples
½ cup broken cashew nuts
½ cup maple-flavored syrup
¼ cup butter or margarine, melted

Wash squash; cut in half lengthwise. Scoop out seeds and stringy substance. Wash, core, and dice unpared apples. Combine with remaining ingredients. Fill squash halves with apple mixture. Brush surface with additional melted butter or margarine. Put in baking dish and pour in boiling water to depth of ½ inch. Cover dish with foil and bake in a preheated 400° oven for 45 minutes. Uncover and bake an additional 10 minutes. Use fork to test squash to be sure it is tender.

---

*God calls us in many ways—
How do we answer?*

Beet Apple Salad

1-pound jar pickled sliced beets
2 medium apples, tart
2 T. mayonnaise
2 T. chopped parsley
1 T. sugar
⅛ t. salt
ground pepper

Drain beets and cut in strips ¼ inch thick. Peel apples and dice finely. Mix all ingredients except parsley. Chill and use parsley as a garnish when served.

Home is where you can be silent and still be heard.

Apple Coleslaw

4 cups finely shredded red or
   white cabbage or 2 cups each,
   mixed
1 Red Delicious apple, cored and
   finely shredded
1 4-ounce can pineapple tidbits,
   drained
½ cup heavy cream
½ cup dairy sour cream
3 T. white vinegar
2 t. sugar
¼ t. salt
⅛ t. white pepper
1 Red Delicious apple, cored and
   thinly sliced, vertically
1½ T. fresh lemon juice

In large bowl place shredded cabbage, shredded apple, and pineapple tidbits. Toss to mix well. In small bowl, whip cream, fold in sour cream, vinegar, sugar, salt, and pepper. Toss with cabbage mixture an chill up to 8 hours before serving. Just before serving, dip the pieces of thinly sliced apple in lemon juice and arrange as garnish over the salad.

Autumn Apple Bread

Makes 1 loaf.

¼ cup shortening
⅔ cup sugar
2 eggs beaten
2 cups sifted all-purpose flour
1 t. baking powder
1 t. baking soda
1 t. salt
2 cups coarsely grated peeled raw
   apples
1 T. grated lemon rind
⅔ cup chopped walnuts

Cream shortening and sugar until light and fluffy; beat in eggs. Sift next 4 ingredients. Add alternately with apples to egg mixture. Stir in lemon rind and nuts. Bake in greased and floured loaf pan (9x5x3 inches) in preheated moderate oven 350° for 50 to 60 minutes. Cool before slicing.

Often our severest tensions arise because we demand our loved ones to be perfect.

Fresh Apple Cake

3 eggs
1 ¾ cups sugar
1 cup oil
2 cups flour
1 t. soda
¼ t. salt
1 t. cinnamon
2 cups diced apples
1 cup chopped nuts
1 t. almond extract

Beat eggs; add sugar, oil, and almond extract. Sift and blend in flour, soda, salt, and cinnamon. Fold in apples and nuts. Turn into 13x9x2-inch greased pan. Bake in preheated 350° oven for about 1 hour.

Apple Pandowdy
Makes 4 servings.

3 cups sliced apples
⅓ cup firmly packed dark brown sugar
¼ t. each of ground cinnamon and nutmeg
¼ cup butter or margarine
⅓ cup granulated sugar
1 egg
¾ cup sifted all-purpose flour
¾ t. baking powder
¼ t. salt
⅓ cup milk
cream

Put apples in 1-quart baking dish. Sprinkle with brown sugar and spices. Bake in a preheated moderate oven 375° for 30 minutes, or until apples are soft. Cream butter; gradually add granulated sugar and beat until fluffy. Add egg and beat well. Add sifted dry ingredients alternately with milk, beating until smooth. Spread on cooked apples. Bake for 30 minutes. Serve warm with cream.

The Lord's been good to me
And so I thank the Lord
For giving me the things I need
The wind and the rain
AND THE APPLE SEED
The Lord's been good to me.

The apple is wonderful in all its color and beauty. It is one of the most important and cultivated trees of all the temperate zones. History verifies that the apple has been grown for over three thousand years. This fruit tree may grow up to forty feet tall and may produce fruit for over one hundred years.

It is a fruit that is in legends, science, art, history, and even in Greek mythology it is told that the golden apples were well guarded because they bestowed immortality on those who had them.

Ancient Romans knew and used the apple, and it is noted that at a banquet in 1670 as many as fifty-six kinds of apples were served. The story is also told that Isaac Newton was made aware of the law of gravity when an apple hit him on the head as he sat by the tree.

Our settlers in America included apple seeds in their precious supplies. The apple thrived and was exported to London as long ago as the American Revolution.

Perhaps one of the most familiar stories, though, is about John Chapman, who traveled in the Ohio wilderness, preaching and planting apple seeds along the way. It was no wonder that he earned the affectionate nickname Johnny Appleseed.

We thought it would be intriguing to have an Apple Festival Party and serve everything from appetizer to dessert made with apples. The hostess may do the entire meal, or it may be that the guests coming may contribute the vegetable, salad, bread, and dessert. If you are really adventurous, have each guest bring something without being assigned. There are recipes for apple cranberry fizz, applesauce yeast bread, apple-herb jelly, apple crumble pizza pie, applesauce pumpkin cake, apple sandwiches, apple oatmeal cookies, and on, and on, and on. But whatever menu you come up with, relax and have fun.

Bridal Shower Luncheon

Menu

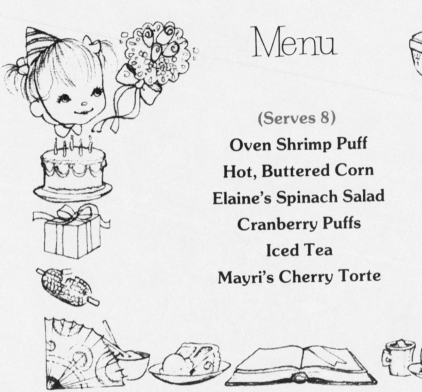

(Serves 8)

Oven Shrimp Puff

Hot, Buttered Corn

Elaine's Spinach Salad

Cranberry Puffs

Iced Tea

Mayri's Cherry Torte

Shortly before my college roommate got married, her mother had a luncheon for the girls who were to be bridesmaids. It was magnificent! I have vivid memories of it still. A beautiful white lace tablecloth, lovely floral centerpiece, and an array of fragile, elegant dishes set the stage for food fit for royalty. The dessert, however, was the most impressive. Each of us received a rose bud "planted" in ice cream which had been covered with chocolate shavings to resemble soil. All this was served in a small clay pot which had been painted and lined with foil. WOW!

You may not choose to do anything quite so elaborate, but a luncheon for a bride-to-be and her friends is one time you can go all out. This meal suits the occasion perfectly. From the very light shrimp puff through the deliciously rich cherry dessert, it's a menu sure to please everyone you invite.

—Carole

Oven Shrimp Puff

10 slices white bread
6 eggs
3 cups milk
2 T. snipped parsley
½ t. dry mustard
½ t. salt
2 cups shredded mild Cheddar
    cheese
3 T. finely chopped onion
3 cups canned shrimp, drained

Heat oven to 325°. Remove crusts from bread. Cut bread into cubes. Beat eggs, milk, and seasonings. Stir in bread cubes, cheese, onion, and shrimp. Pour mixture into an un-greased baking dish. Bake uncovered for 1 hour, or until center is set.

Cranberry Puffs

2 cups cranberry-orange relish
1 cup buttermilk biscuit baking
    mix
½ cup sugar
2 eggs
⅔ cup milk

Heat oven to 400°. Generously grease bottoms of 16 to 18 muffin cups. Spoon about 2 tablespoons cranberry-orange relish into each muffin cup. Blend baking mix, sugar, eggs, and milk, beating vigorously for ½ minute. Fill muffin cups ⅔ full. Bake about 15 minutes, or until golden. Invert puffs onto wire rack. Serve warm with butter sauce.

Butter Sauce
½ cup sugar
¼ cup light cream
¼ cup butter or margarine
½ t. vanilla

Heat sugar and light cream to boiling, stirring constantly. Remove from heat. With a rotary beater, beat in butter or margarine and vanilla.

Hint: Bake oven shrimp puff first; then raise heat in oven and bake cranberry puffs. Cover oven shrimp puff to keep it hot while cranberry puffs bake.

Elaine's Spinach Salad

1 10-ounce package fresh spinach
1 head lettuce
½ bottle of bacon bits
6 hard-boiled eggs, chopped
8 fresh spring onions, chopped
1 box frozen peas, cooked as
   directed and cooled

The night before serving wash and dry the vegetables well. Place all the salad ingredients in a large bowl in the order listed. Mix dressing.

Dressing
2 cups mayonnaise
1 cup sour cream
1 package Hidden Valley Ranch
   Dressing

Spread dressing over the salad as icing. Cover and refrigerate overnight. Stir when ready to serve.

Mayri's Cherry Torte

Crust
3 egg whites
1 t. vanilla
1 cup sugar
¾ cup walnuts
½ cup salted crushed saltines
   (about 14 crackers)
1 t. baking powder

Filling
1 cup (½ pint) whipping cream

Topping
1 20-ounce can cherry pie filling

Make crust by beating egg whites and vanilla until foamy. Add sugar gradually and beat to stiff peaks. Mix walnuts, saltines, and baking powder together. Fold into egg whites. Spread into a well-greased 9-inch pie pan, building up the sides Bake at 300° about 40 minutes, or until dry on the outside. Cool.

Whip cream until stiff. Fill crust with whipped cream. Cover with pie filling. Dollop remaining whipped cream on top. Cut into 8 pieces after thoroughly chilling.

Children's Birthday Party

Menu

(Serves 6)

Individual Pizzas

Assorted Munchies

Pretzels, Popcorn, Cheese Puffs,

Potato Chips, and so forth

Fruity Punch

Ice Cream Pie

Birthdays are so much fun! One tradition when I was growing up was letting the birthday boy or girl choose what foods were served for supper. Another tradition was the annual party.

Now it's my turn to give parties for my children. I have discovered a few tips which I find helpful when "Party Time" rolls around: (1) With young children, have plenty of disposable washcloths and paper towels handy as there's bound to be at least one spill; (2) Use a cookie with each child's name written in icing as a placecard for each guest; (3) Be prepared to be songleader, photographer, waitress, referee, games director, and more unless you assign these jobs to someone else beforehand; and (4) Remember it's really not *your* party, so include your child in much of the planning and carrying out off the festivities. You'll both enjoy it more.

—Carole

Ice Cream Pie

Note: The beauty of this dessert for a child's birthday party is that it can be custom-made for the child. Let him or her decide which kind of crust, which flavor ice cream, and what kind of topping to use. Following are a few suggestions:

Chocolate Cookie Crust

1½ cups chocolate wafer crumbs
6 T. butter or margarine, melted

Mix together crumbs and butter. Press firmly into a 9-inch pie plate. Chill until set, at least 1 hour.

Graham Cracker Crust

1¼ cups fine graham cracker crumbs
¼ cup sugar
6 T. butter or margarine, melted

Combine ingredients. Press firmly into a 9-inch pie plate. Chill at least 45 minutes before filling.

Coconut Crust

1 3½-ounce can flaked coconut (1⅓ cups)
2 T. melted butter or margarine

Combine coconut and butter. Press into a 9-inch pie pan. Bake at 325° for 15 minutes, or until coconut is light brown.

Filling

Use 1 quart of any flavor ice ceam. Let it soften at room temperature just until it is easy to spoon into chilled pie crust. Then cover and put entire pie in freezer. Chill until firm. Remove pie from freezer several minutes before serving to facilitate cutting. Don't forget to put birthday candles on it!

Topping

Use one jar of any flavor ice-cream topping or make your own praline sauce or fudge sauce. Pour topping on each piece after cutting or on the entire pie before cutting.

Fudge Sauce

Makes 3 cups.

1 14½-ounce can evaporated milk
2 cups sugar
4-ounce unsweetened chocolate
¼ cup butter or margarine
1 t. vanilla
½ t. salt

Heat milk and sugar to boiling, stirring constantly. Boil and stir 1 minute. Add chocolate. Stir until it melts. Beat over heat until smooth—you may need to beat vigorously. Remove from heat. Add vanilla, butter, and salt; mix gently.

Keep a list of your friends and let God be first on the list however long it may be.

Praline Sauce

Makes 1 cup.

¼ cup butter or margarine
½ cup powdered sugar
2 T. maple syrup
¼ cup water
½ t. vanilla
½ cup finely chopped pecans

Heat butter over medium heat until golden. Cool. Slowly add sugar, mixing until smooth. Stir in syrup and water. Heat to boiling. Boil and stir 1 minute. Cool slightly. Stir in vanilla and nuts. This thickens as it cools.

Fruity Punch

1 6-ounce can frozen grape juice concentrate
1 12-ounce can frozen orange juice concentrate
3 to 4 cups water (to taste)
1 6-ounce can unsweetened apple juice

Mix all ingredients well. Add a little sugar if needed. Float orange slices on top when serving.

Individual Pizzas

3 10-count flaky refrigerator biscuits
¾ cup tomato paste
3 t. oregano
1 t. basil
⅛ t. garlic powder
1½ to 2 cups shredded mozzarella cheese

Preheat oven to 400°. Grease baking sheets. Pat each biscuit into a 4-inch circle on baking sheets. Mix tomato paste and spices; brush on each biscuit round. Top with shredded cheese. Bake until crust is lightly browned—approximately 8 minutes.

Note: Other ingredients such as cooked ground beef or sausage, pepperoni, chopped green pepper, onions, or mushrooms can be placed on tomato paste mixture and topped with cheese before baking.

The earth is a garden and we are the caretakers.

Bacon, an old French word meaning "pork," has been around for a long time. But bacon pigs, capable of producing the tasty bacon we enjoy, weren't developed until this last century. Thus, the early pioneers who trekked across the country moving west with their hogs ate stringy bacon and tough pork.

There's an interesting correlation between spices and the founding of Yale University. Because early Americans lacked proper refrigeration, they often had to mask off-flavors in their meats with the abundant use of **spices.** Thus spices became a big selling item with cooks everywhere. Black pepper was an especially popular and lucrative spice. One man, Elihu Yale, made his fortune selling black pepper and went on to use his wealth to start the Ivy League university named for him.

In the early 1800s the Reverend Sylvester Graham traveled throughout the United States sharing his thoughts on nutrition. He encouraged the use of coarse cereals in the diet, along with fruits and vegetables. He even opened shops that sold "Graham-approved" foods. But he is best known for one food he gave us—the **graham cracker.**

Many of us are always on the lookout for good Sunday meals. We want something special and yet something easy to prepare after church. The colonists in the 1700s must have had the same wishes, coupled with stringent restrictions against working on Sunday. Therefore, they enjoyed dishes like **Boston baked beans** because they could be made ahead, served fresh on Saturday, and then eaten either hot or cold at noontime on Sunday.

During the Civil War, many soldiers found **coffee** to be the most important ration. As soon as a campfire could be kindled, the soldiers began brewing the coffee they'd been issued. Along with the coffee, they were given sugar, and the men learned to mix the two together at once before the sugar could get wet, spilled, or stolen. Army life introduced coffee to many men who had never seen it before, and after the war it became America's national drink.

The first American settlers found **soups** to be what we now call "convenience foods." Women often kept leftover soup simmering on the fire after a meal. Then every day they added other meats and vegetables so that there was always hot and ready soup to eat.

Chinese Progressive

Dinner Party

Menu

(Serves 6)

Egg Drop Soup   Egg Rolls

Shrimp Toast

Fried Rice

Sweet 'n Sour Chicken

Chinese Pepper Steak

Almond Angels

Frozen Mandarin Oranges

Tea

American appreciation of the Oriental food received its impetus from Chinese restaurants.

Respect for food caused the Chinese to perfect stir-frying. It is fun to watch an Oriental cook arrange the sliced meat and vegetables around the large shallow pan called the wok. The oil is carefully heated and the ingredients added at just the right moment while stirring continually. Then the food is deftly lifted to the serving dish. To Oriental cooks, the appearance of a dish is just as important as the flavor.

When entertaining, care is taken to be sure that the Chinese dishes served all have different color, texture, and basic flavor. Often nuts, fruits or soups are served between the courses to clear the palate. Again the one word here is, "enjoy!"

—Cindy

Egg Drop Soup
Makes 6 cups.

6 cups boiling water
6 chicken bouillon cubes
3 eggs
6 T. chopped scallions

Put water and bouillon cubes in a saucepan. Simmer until the cubes are dissolved. While that is simmering in a small bowl beat the eggs. Slowly pour the eggs into the broth, stirring constantly. Simmer for 1 minute. Serve topped with scallions. This recipe may be made twice for a large group (or however many servings are needed), but it does better if it is not doubled.

Shrimp Toast
Makes 24 appetizers.

1 pound frozen, shelled, and deveined shrimp, cooked and chilled
24 slices party rye bread or white bread cut without the crusts
1 cup mayonnaise or salad dressing
½ cup shredded Cheddar cheese
dash of curry powder
dash of paprika

Chop the shrimp finely or put into a food processor. Mix the shrimp, mayonnaise, cheese, and curry powder. Spread some of the mixture over the bread. Sprinkle with paprika. Place on a cookie sheet and put in a preheated broiler 3 to 4 inches from the heat. Broil about 1 to 2 minutes, or until the topping starts to bubble. Serve at once.

Home should be clean enough to be healthy but dirty enough to be happy.

Egg Rolls Filling

3 cups finely chopped, cooked chicken, pork, or shrimp (or you can combine pork and shrimp or any combination)

2 cups finely chopped celery

1 cup finely chopped green onions

1 small can chopped water chestnuts

Mix the above ingredients with the following:

1 T. monosodium glutamate

1 T. soy sauce

2 t. sugar

1 t. salt

1 egg

¼ cup melted margarine

1 garlic clove, minced

Put the filling in a large bowl and refrigerate while you make the skins.*

Egg Roll Skins

1 ⅓ cups flour

⅔ cup cornstarch

½ cup water

Sift the dry ingredients together and gradually add the water. Blend well.

Add one cup more water gradually, beating until smooth. Reserve ⅓ of batter. Heat the skillet and brush with oil. Pour 2 tablespoons of the batter into the skillet. Tilt the pan to make a round pancake. Cook until the mixture looks dry. Do not turn. Stack the skins until the batter is finished.

Place a teaspoon of the filling on the cooked side of each skin and fold or wrap. Fry in about 1 inch of hot oil 5 to 8 minutes, turning once. Use a little batter to hold the egg rolls together. These can be made ahead, cooled, then frozen. To reheat, bake them at 400° for 20 minutes.

*If you prefer not to make your own skins, buy the wontons in the supermarket and use the egg roll filling. The only difference is that the wontons tend to be a little larger than the homemade skins and a tablespoon of filling seems to be better. The cooking instructions are the same. You may want to use a little water to help the wontons stick together. This recipe makes between 50 to 60 egg rolls. You may need to double the skin recipe, but the filling is ample.

Fried Rice

2 cups rice
8 slices bacon, fried crisp
½ cup thinly sliced water
   chestnuts
½ cup finely sliced bamboo shoots
½ cup minced onions (or ½ cup
   scallions)
½ cup finely diced green pepper
1 T. soy sauce
peanut oil

Cook the rice according to directions on the box. Heat the oil in a large skillet and add all the ingredients except the rice. Cook over a medium heat for 10 minutes, stirring constantly. Add the rice and cook until very hot. May be doubled.

Chinese Pepper Steak

Makes 4 to 6 servings.

2 T. peanut (or cooking) oil
1 pound round steak, cut into thin
   strips*
2 T. minced onion
1 clove garlic, minced
2 green peppers, cut into strips
½ cup sliced celery
½ cup beef consommé
2 t. water
2 T. cornstarch
1 t. soy sauce
salt and pepper to taste
4 cups cooked rice

*The meat will slice more easily if it is slightly frozen (put in the freezer section for about ½ hour).

Heat the oil in a skillet or electric frying pan. Add the beef and brown over a medium heat. Add the onion, garlic, peppers, celery, and consommé; season with salt and pepper. Cover; simmer for 30 minutes. Combine the water, cornstarch, and soy sauce. Stir in the meat mixture; simmer for 5 minutes. Serve over noodles.

Sweet 'n Sour Chicken

Serves 6.

1 egg
2 ½ cups cut-up cooked chicken
¼ cup cornstarch
2 T. shortening
1 15¼-ounce can pineapple
  chunks (drain and reserve
  syrup)
½ cup vinegar
½ cup sugar
1 medium green pepper, finely
  chopped
¼ cup water
2 T. cornstarch
1 t. soy sauce
1 1-pound can small carrots,
  drained

Toss the chicken in the beaten egg and sprinkle with ¼ cup cornstarch. Cook the chicken in melted shortening until brown. Remove from skillet. Add enough water to reserved pineapple syrup to make 1 cup. Stir the liquid, vinegar, and sugar into the skillet. Heat to boiling, stirring constantly.

Add green pepper; heat to boiling. Reduce heat; cover and simmer for 2 or 3 minutes.

Blend the water and 2 tablespoons cornstarch. Stir into the mixture in the skillet. Cook, stirring constantly until thickened and boiling. Boil and stir 1 minute. Stir in the pineapple, soy sauce, carrots, and chicken. Heat. Serve over rice.

If God has blessed you, tell it;
If God has given to you, use it.

Almond Angels

Makes 3½ to 4 dozen cookies.

4 egg whites
¼ t. cream of tartar
¼ t. salt
1¾ cups sugar
½ t. vanilla
½ t. almond extract
¾ cup blanched slivered almonds

Combine the egg whites, cream of tartar, and salt; beat until the mixture holds soft peaks. Gradually beat in sugar, then flavorings; fold in almonds. Grease cookie sheets well. Line with brown paper and grease the paper well. Drop the mixture by teaspoonfuls onto greased paper. Bake at 250° degrees for 50 minutes. Remove from the cookie sheet immediately and cool on wire racks. Makes approximately 3½ to 4 dozen cookies.

If we must have patience and endurance, let it be with joy!

Frozen Mandarin Oranges

This offers a nice end to a Chinese meal. The number of cans of oranges needed will depend on the number of people to be invited. Drain the oranges and place them on a cookie sheet in the freezer for about 1 hour. Serve immediately.

Tea

Green tea is the tea traditionally served with a Chinese meal. You may wish to try this, but I would suggest having some other types available. Constant Comment with its orange flavor would go well.

If you have never participated in a Progressive Party, this would be a good time to get initiated. It doesn't require much work for any one person and is fun to go to different homes during the evening. Our Sunday school class had a Chinese dinner party, and it was one of the most popular social events we have had. We planned ours to coincide with the Chinese New Year. This date varies each year but usually is in February. You could check the date and then plan your party for the Friday or Saturday night that comes closest to the actual date. We also gave shiny new pennies in red envelopes as favors. This is a sign of good luck to the Chinese.

One of the fun requirements at the party is to request everyone to eat with chopsticks. Of course, it is good to have forks for those who are not comfortable with chopsticks, but part of the fun is learning a new skill and laughing with everyone.

Three homes seem to work well for this party. Have the appetizers at one home, the main course at another, and the desserts and tea (also serve coffee for those who prefer it) at the last home. The weather at this time of year may not be the best, so attempt to plan the homes fairly close together. It is also a good idea to have everyone prepare something. They should take it ahead of time to the home where it is to be served. This allows the hostess time to get it reheated and put it in serving dishes and it eliminates carrying dishes between homes the evening of the party.

Perhaps you and a friend could make the egg rolls. The recipe in the menu for the dinner is for homemade egg rolls, but an easier way is to buy the skins. They are usually found in the produce section of your grocery, or can be ordered ahead of time. One other item that would be a big help (if you have one) is a food processor. It can chop the vegetables and meat so fine that there is very little work involved in making the egg rolls. A good sharp knife, a cutting board, and some "elbow grease" will be fine if you don't have a processor.

Usually, along with the meal, someone may plan a brief game or bit of entertainment at each home with the main theme of the program being presented at the last home.

—Cindy

Down South Meal

Menu

(Serves 6)

Fruit Cup

Fried Chicken with Cream Gravy

Fried Corn off the Cob   **Fried Okra**

Candied Sweet Potatoes

Sliced Tomatoes, Bread and Butter Pickles

Hot Buttermilk Biscuits, Fresh Peach Preserves

Pineapple Cream Pie or Vinegar Pie

Pralines   **Beverages**

People on the move often take with them their favorite recipes. My parents did this when they left Texas to return to Tennessee only to be on the move again in a few years. Southern style cooking was an important part of the home. Some of the recipes that mama used were written, but many were not, so the tradition passed on to us had to be learned by watching mama in the kitchen. Biscuits for breakfast every morning accompanied the fried eggs and milk gravy. This was followed with jelly or sorgum and butter on a piping hot biscuit. What a way to begin a day!

But how much is a "pinch," or a "smidgin," or a "whoa, that's enough"? How does one deftly shape a well in the mound of flour in the round wooden bowl and mix with the fingers until it is just the "right" consistency? Biscuit making was a culinary art with mama as were the other ways of Southern cooking we enjoyed in childhood.

—Elizabeth

Fruit Cup

1 cup frozen peaches
1 cup frozen strawberries
1 sliced banana
1 can chilled mandarin oranges
1 diced fresh apple
½ cup frozen blueberries

Mix all together, putting in blueberries at last minute. Serve as appetizer with crisp crackers. For the real Southern tradition, a light custard is poured over the fruit. It may be a real ambrosia with a little coconut also added.

Candied Sweet Potatoes

2 large sweet potatoes
2 T. butter
2 T. water
½ cup sugar
cinnamon, to taste

Peel sweet potatoes and slice about ¼ inch thick. Put into heavy skillet with butter and water. Cover and let steam until tender, about 10 minutes. Add sugar and cinnamon to taste. Take lid off when blended and let simmer. It is best not to stir.

Fried Okra

2 cups sliced okra, frozen or fresh
¼ cup flour
¼ cup cornmeal
salt and pepper to taste

Cut off top of okra; slice and toss with other ingredients. Fry in hot grease for about 15 minutes, turning often. This is a must for any real Southern meal and very different from any recipe calling for boiled okra.

Pineapple Cream Pie

⅓ cup flour
⅔ cup sugar
¼ t. salt
2 cups milk
3 slightly beaten egg yolks
2 T. butter or margarine
½ cup drained crushed pineapple
½ t. vanilla
1 9 inch baked pie shell
3 stiffly beaten egg whites
4 T. sugar

Mix flour, sugar, and salt. Add milk and egg yolks. Cook until thick, stirring often. Add butter and vanilla. Drain pineapple very well and add last. Pour into baked shell and cover with meringue made of egg whites and sugar. Bake in moderate oven until meringue browns.

Faith is the main stimulus in a Christian's life.

Pralines

1 cup firmly packed light brown
  sugar
1 cup granulated sugar
⅔ cup evaporated milk
½ t. vanilla
1½ cups pecan halves

In heavy saucepan, combine sugars and milk; cook, stirring constantly with wooden spoon until soft ball stage is reached, 234° to 238°. Remove from heat; stir in vanilla and pecans. Immediately drop by tablespoonfuls onto buttered cookie sheet.

Vinegar Pie

2 cups boiling water
¼ cup vinegar
1 cup sugar
3 T. cornstarch
3 eggs, separated
2 T. butter
1 t. lemon flavoring
½ t. salt
6 T. sugar
baked pie shell

Beat egg yolks until thick. Add sugar, cornstarch, and salt. Mix thoroughly. Boil together water and vinegar and add slowly to dry ingredients, stirring constantly. Boil until mixture is thick and smooth. Add lemon flavoring and butter. Pour into baked pie shell and cover with meringue made with 3 egg whites and 6 tablespoons of sugar. Brown meringue in moderate oven at 350° for about 12 minutes, or until lightly browned.

Grandparents are for fun—yes, they are. They are one of God's most delightful creations.

Parents, of necessity, have to engage in the serious business of child rearing. It may be difficult, since it is the first go-round for them, but grandparents can enter that fantasy-land of make believe with the child. They seem to see and hear with more understanding hearts than parents.

Our three little grandsons, Todd, Stephen, and Mark, are real ego-builders. When they come to "papa's house" they tell their parents, "I could stay at papa's forever." They take walks with us and in the early evening pretend to reach and touch the moon. They are stimulus for tired blood when in all sincerity they say, "Grandmama do it."

There is a special bond as we share the mysteries of birds, flowers, and the squiggly worms. We may be mutual pals in mischief. We marvel at their unrestrained innocence and their freedom to express themselves. How can we ever forget saying to Todd, "My, but you are such a fine boy," and with true humility his reply came quickly, "I sure are." Or Stephen after a rough day turning to his mother and explaining it all by saying, "'I need to be cranky." And at this writing little Mark is just beginning to wrinkle his eyes and pucker his mouth and make a wonderful sound that I am sure says, "I love you, too."

Grandparents are an extension of the nuclear family and even make good baby-sitters. You don't have to be rich or famous, you need only a childlike quality of life. In this world of complex rules and regulations grandparents can be a court of appeals. When parental discipline seems hard to take, our little guys have learned to preface their plight with a "I go to papa's house." They know full well that they will get an unbiased hearing of their case, plus a big hug and a visit to the cookie jar. We are not overruling parental decisions but are creating such a pleasant diversion that tears are soon forgotten.

God must have had a special purpose in creating grandparents. They may be a gentle buffer between the tender world of childhood and the real world—a sort of extension of God's love.

Yes, grandparents are for fun.

—Elizabeth

Fireside Dinner for Two

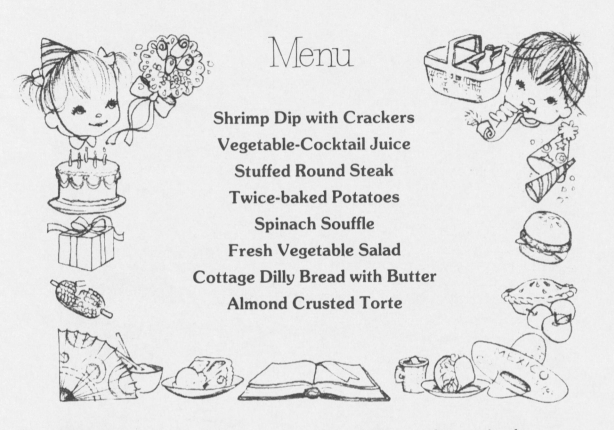

Menu

Shrimp Dip with Crackers

Vegetable-Cocktail Juice

Stuffed Round Steak

Twice-baked Potatoes

Spinach Souffle

Fresh Vegetable Salad

Cottage Dilly Bread with Butter

Almond Crusted Torte

Going out to dinner can be great!
But what if the car won't start
Or the sitter is late?
The steak is burned and
The shrimp are limp.
The service is slow
And you wonder why you go.
Then a fireside dinner for two
Could be just the evening for you.
After the children are in bed
Much can be said
For the quiet evening ahead.
So put a log on the fire,
And pick up your spoon—
Dinner for two will be ready soon.
—Cindy

Stuffed Round Steak

Makes 2 to 3 generous servings or 4 smaller servings.

½ onion, finely chopped
1 4-ounce can sliced mushrooms, drained
1 T. melted margarine
⅛ t. thyme
⅛ t. sage
1 round steak (¾ to 1 pound)
½ to ¾ cup bread crumbs
salt and pepper to taste
four
salad oil
¼ cup water

Sauté onions and mushrooms in margarine; add bread crumbs, thyme, and sage, stirring well. Season steak with salt and pepper; spread with bread crumb mixture. Roll up steak and fasten with skewers; dredge in flour. Brown in hot oil; add water. Cover and bake at 325° for 45 minutes, or until meat is tender.

Shrimp Dip

1 stick butter
1 8-ounce package cream cheese, softened
1 T. mayonnaise
1 t. lemon juice
1 4-ounce can cocktail shrimp, drained
dash garlic salt
1 t. grated onion

Beat the ingredients with a mixer. Chill and serve with crackers. This makes quite a bit more than just for two, but it keeps well and will taste good if company drops in unexpectedly.

Twice-baked Potatoes

1 large baking potato, baked
1 T. butter or margarine
¼ cup milk (start with a little less)
¼ t. salt
¼ cup grated cheese
paprika to taste

Preheat oven to 375°. Cut the potatoes in half lengthwise; scoop out pulp, leaving thin shells. Whip pulp with butter and milk until light and fluffy. Add salt; pile into the two shells. Put on a baking sheet and sprinkle with cheese. Bake in a preheated oven for 15 minutes. Sprinkle with paprika just before serving.

Spinach Souffle

¼ cup butter or margarine
1 T. grated onion
5 T. flour
1 cup milk
1 cup grated Cheddar cheese
1 cup cooked chopped spinach
1 t. salt
dash of pepper
3 eggs, separated

Preheat the oven to 350°. Grease a 1½-quart casserole dish. Melt the butter or margarine in a saucepan; add the onion and sauté for 5 minutes. Blend in the flour. Gradually stir in the milk, and cook over a medium heat, stirring constantly until thickened and smooth. Remove from heat. Stir in cheese, spinach, salt, and pepper. In a mixing bowl, beat the egg yolks until thick and lemon colored. In another mixing bowl beat the egg whites until stiff (but not dry). Carefully fold the egg whites and yolks into the cheese mixture. Pour into the casserole and bake for 45 minutes, or until a knife inserted in the middle comes out clean.

Fresh Vegetable Salad

1 head cauliflower
1 bunch broccoli
1 small carton cherry tomatoes
1 small can pitted black olives,
   drained
1 large bottle Italian salad dressing

Wash the cauliflower, broccoli, and cherry tomatoes. Drain on paper towels. Pull the cauliflower and broccoli apart into flowerets. In a large bowl add the tomatoes, ripe olives, and the cauliflower and broccoli flowerets. Pour the salad dressing over the vegetables and refrigerate overnight. This makes a large salad but will keep for several days and can make a nice salad for company.

Cottage Dilly Bread

1 package dry yeast
¼ cup warm water
1 cup cottage cheese
2 t. dill weed
¼ t. soda
1 unbeaten egg
1 T. melted butter or margarine
½ T. minced onion
2 T. sugar
2½ cups flour

Preheat the oven to 350°. Dissolve the yeast in the warm water and set aside. Combine in a large bowl all of the ingredients except the yeast mixture and flour. After thoroughly mixing, add the yeast mixture and flour. Let rise in a greased bowl to double the size. Punch down. Put in one 9x5-inch well-greased bread pan. Let rise again, about 45 to 50 minutes. Bake for about 30 minutes. Remove from pan and brush with melted margarine.

When another person can hurt me, I have room for improvement.

Almond Crusted Torte

½ **cup butter or margarine**
1 **cup flour**
½ **cup sugar**
½ **cup chopped, slivered almonds,
   toasted**
1 **cup chilled whipping cream**
1 **quart chocolate ice cream**
1 **t. rum extract**

*Melt butter in a large skillet; stir in
flour, sugar, and almonds. Cook over
a medium heat, stirring constantly until
mixture is golden and crumbly (about
6 to 8 minutes.) Save ¾ cup of the
crumb mixture. Pat the remaining
crumb mixture into a buttered 9-inch
springform pan. Freeze at least 3
hours. Beat the cream in a chilled
small mixer bowl until soft peaks form.
Soften the ice cream slightly in a large
bowl. Gently add the extract and
whipped cream to the ice-cream
mixture. Spoon into the crumb-lined
pan. Freeze until partially set, about 1
hour. Sprinkle with reserved crumbs.*

*Store in the freezer and freeze until
firm (about 2 hours). This will keep
for about 1½ weeks in your freezer;
however, if you are going to make it
or keep it for this long, be sure it is
tightly covered.*

*When you are lonely, I wish you love.
When you are down, I wish you joy.*

Make Mine Mexican

Menu

(Serves 8)

Hot Bean Dip with Corn Chips

Chicken Enchiladas

Mexican Corn Relish Salad

Spanish Rice

Sopaipillas

Fresh Fruit Plate

Chocolate Meringues

Mexican Coffee

Get out the bright paper flowers, colorful tablecloth, some stoneware dishes and have a fiesta! Mexican food and a happy, exciting atmosphere just seem to go hand in hand, so plan a fun evening with some of your friends.

More and more people are discovering how tasty tacos, frijoles, enchiladas, and tamales are; and you can treat your guests to a grand sampling of Mexican cuisine using this menu. Don't let the thought of hot spices keep you from trying these foods. Simply season them moderately (as the recipes suggest), and then provide extra chili powder and hot peppers for those whose tastes are more adventuresome.

Spanish Rice

1 small green pepper, chopped
3 T. margarine
2 cups white rice (not minute rice)
2 cups water
2 cups tomato juice
2 t. salt

Sauté green pepper in melted butter for 3 to 5 minutes. Cook rice as directed on package, using combination of tomato juice and water rather than all water. During final 5 minutes of cooking time, add green pepper to rice. Serve hot.

Hot Bean Dip

1 15-ounce can refried beans
2 T. milk
2 ounces (½ cup) shredded
   Monterey Jack cheese
corn chips

Mix beans and milk in saucepan. Heat, stirring constantly. Add cheese. Cook and stir until cheese melts. Serve in a chafing dish or fondue pot to keep warm and of good consistency. Dip with corn chips.

Chicken Enchiladas

12 to 14 chicken breasts
3 small cans chopped olives
24 to 30 flour tortillas
3 12-ounce blocks of Monterey
   Jack cheese, shredded

Sauce
2 onions, chopped
4 T. salad oil
3 15-ounce cans tomato sauce
1 T. salt
2 cloves garlic, minced
2 t. ground cumin seed
½ t. oregano
3 cans enchilada sauce

Cook chicken in a 350° oven for 45 minutes (covered). Bone, skin, and shred into small pieces. Add one can of chopped olives and enough sauce to moisten. Fry tortillas in hot oil for 5 seconds on each side. Put some of the chicken mixture and some cheese in the middle of each tortilla and roll. Fasten with toothpicks and place seam side down in baking dish. Cover with remaining sauce. Sprinkle with remaining cheese and olives. Bake, covered, for 25 minutes at 350°.

Sauce: Sauté onion in oil until limp, but not brown. Stir in remaining ingredients. Simmer 45 minutes.

*Some people seem to be born old,
and some never grow old.*

Mexican Corn Relish Salad

½ cup mayonnaise
¼ cup minced green onions
2 T. chili sauce
1 t. onion salt
2 t. vinegar
½ t. chili powder
3-4 drops hot pepper sauce
1 15-ounce can Mexican corn
1 15-ounce can red kidney beans
1 7-ounce can pitted ripe olives
2 cups shredded lettuce

Mix first seven ingredients for dressing. Cover and chill. Drain and combine corn, beans, and olives. Line a salad bowl with lettuce and spoon in corn mixture. Serve with dressing.

Chocolate Meringues

3 egg whites
¼ t. cream of tartar
¾ cup sugar
1 cup chilled whipping cream
½ cup chocolate fudge topping
½ t. vanilla
½ cup chopped nuts

Beat egg whites and cream of tartar until foamy. Slowly beat in sugar, continuing until stiff and glossy. Drop meringue by ⅓ cupfuls onto a cookie sheet covered with brown paper. Shape mounds of meringue into eight 3-inch circles, building up the sides. Bake 1 hour at 275°. Turn off oven and leave meringues in oven with door closed for another 1½ hours. Remove and cool away from draft. Beat cream until soft peaks form. Beat in fudge topping and vanilla on low speed. Fold in nuts. Spread about ¼ cup of this filling on each cooled meringue shell. Freeze, uncovered, until filling is firm, about 3 hours. (May be frozen for up to a week.)

Sopaipillas
Makes 18.

1 cup flour
1½ t. baking powder
½ salt
½ t. sugar
1 T. shortening
⅓ cup warm water

Mix together the first four ingredients. Cut in shortening until the consistency of cornmeal. Add water and stir until it becomes a stiff dough. Turn into a floured surface and knead 5 minutes. Put in a bowl and let stand 20 minutes. Roll dough to an 18x6-inch rectangle. Cut pieces 2x3-inches. Slide several pieces into hot (375°) oil that has been heated in a heavy saucepan. Fry one layer at a time for about 1 minute on each side, or until golden and puffed. Lift out with a slotted spoon and drain on paper towels. Repeat with remaining dough. Serve warm with honey or powdered sugar.

If you want to prepare these a day ahead, let them cool after frying. Put them in a plastic bag at room temperature. Then reheat them in a single layer on a cookie sheet at 250° for 8 to 10 minutes

Mexican Coffee

4 cups water
½ cup packed dark brown sugar
1 cinnamon stick
4 whole cloves
¼ cup regular grind coffee

Heat water, sugar, cinnamon, and cloves in saucepan. Stir until sugar is dissolved. Add coffee. Heat to boiling; then reduce heat and simmer uncovered for 2 minutes. Stir; cover saucepan. Heat on low heat a few minutes, until grounds settle. Strain and serve in demitasse cups.

Our freedom is a priceless commodity; but is blemished when we fail to exercise our rights as citizens.

Today people are increasingly interested in naturally grown foods without chemicals being used in preserving these foods. Many who have their own gardens are turning to the ways of the past and old methods of growing certain foods. Food companies also are looking for health foods in the histories of past civilizations. Recently, one such company marketed a new bread with ingredients that they claimed were taken from a passage in the Bible.

Many references are found in the Old and New Testament to foods, feasts, gardens, fields, and the eating habits of people. Indeed, food was an important aspect of life for the ancients just as it is for us today. In the Bible, one of the main forms of wealth was the crop that was raised. Growing, trading, and preparing foods are listed as main occupations in the Bible. The topic of food was used frequently in Jesus' teachings and parables.

With great interest one reads of Abraham's journey into Canaan and of the figs, grapes, and other kinds of fruit he found there. We learn, too, of

Joseph's life in Egypt and of the dates, cucumbers, beans, carrots, lettuce, and meats flavored with onion and garlic that they enjoyed.

When the Israelites left Egypt they journeyed toward the Promised Land but sorely missed their melons, leeks, cucumbers, and onions (Num. 11:5). Ruth worked in the barley fields. When David hid from King Saul he was sent parched grain, loaves of bread, and cheese. Ezekiel "took of the seed of the land and planted it in fertile soil; he placed it beside the abundant waters" (Ezek. 17:5).

It can tie us more closely together when we know that many of the Bible gardens included the same kinds of fruits and vegetables we enjoy today. About the only basic foods that were not known to the Bible land people were corn, citrus fruit, mushrooms, tomatoes, and potatoes.

Along with the fruits and vegetables in the Bible gardens were a variety of herbs that we use today such as sage, mustard, parsley, and mint. And it is highly probable that some of the Bible gardens included a decorative touch with flowers and vines. But for the average family of that time, it was a no-nonsense approach to food

planting and reaping. They planned, planted, and cultivated their gardens. Ours is an easier life for the preserving, canning, and freezing the fruits of our labor, but we are not any happier than they were as they celebrated their harvest with joy and gratitude.

We have a kinship with our Bible friends through our gardens.

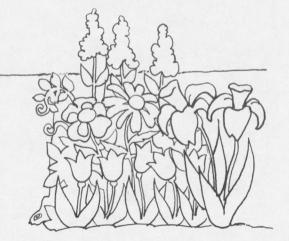

Old-Fashioned
Sunday Dinner

Menu

(Serves 6 to 8)

Roast Pork with Gravy

Potatoes Browned with the Roast

Apple and Yam Casserole

Frozen Peas with Sliced Mushrooms

Cucumber Salad   **Corn Sticks with Butter**

Fudge Pie

Coffee, Tea, Milk

Sunday dinner, after church, is for many people a special tradition that has been passed down from family to family.

I'll always remember the zestful aroma of roast beef baking in the oven on Sunday as we'd come home from church. It took much more doing than I realized at the time.

With good help from all family members (helping may mean entertaining the little ones by keeping them out of the kitchen) this menu can be ready shortly after everyone is home from church. The salad can be made the night before; the roast put in a low oven before church, adding the peeled and quartered potatoes the minute you get home. The casserole and corn sticks may be baked at the same time. Then the peas, coffee or tea and finishing touches to the table may be done. The pie (served warm) can cook while the family is eating dinner. Enjoy your dinner.

Roast Pork with Gravy

Serves 6 to 8.

3 ½ pounds pork loin
1 T. chopped onion
2 T. flour
1 t. salt
¼ t. pepper
½ t. liquid seasoning for gravy
spices to taste (if desired)

Preheat the oven to 325°. Place the pork (fat side up) in a roasting pan. Season with a light sprinkling of salt and pepper. Roast 2 hours. Remove to a heated platter and keep warm. Also remove the potatoes and put them in a separate dish (see following recipe). Add 1 tablespoon of fat to the pan (after removing the fat and leaving the meat juices). Add the onions and sauté them. Remove from the heat and stir in the 2 tablespoons of flour to form a smooth mixture; then stir in the rest of the ingredients. Gradually add 1½ cups water, bring to a boil, stirring until thickened and smooth.

Simmer briefly. Serve with the potatoes and roast.

Potatoes with the Roast

6 to 8 baking potatoes, peeled, washed, and cut into quarters

The quarters of the potatoes should be placed around the roast the last hour of baking.

Frozen Peas with Sliced Mushrooms

2 10-ounce packages frozen peas
1 small jar sliced mushrooms
    (drained) or several fresh large
    mushrooms sliced

Cook the peas according to the package directions. During the last few minutes of cooking add the mushrooms. Serve piping hot! May be dotted with butter just before serving.

Apple and Yam Casserole

1 21-ounce can apple pie filling
2 17-ounce cans whole sweet
    potatoes, drained
3 T. butter
¼ t. nutmeg
½ cup chopped nuts (walnuts or
    pecans work best)

Preheat the oven to 325°. Combine the pie filling and sweet potatoes, placing them in a buttered 7x11-inch baking dish. Dot with 3 tablespoons butter; sprinkle lightly with the nutmeg and chopped nuts. Bake 30 minutes, or until bubbly.

*"By wisdom a house is built,
and by understanding
it is established"*
(Prov. 24:3).

Cucumber Salad

Serves 12.

2 3-ounce packages lime Jell-O
2 t. finely chopped green pepper
2 t. chopped onion
2 t. chopped carrot
2 t. chopped cucumber
1 8-ounce carton cottage cheese

Prepare the Jell-O as directed, but use only three cups of water (1½ cups of boiling water and 1½ cups of cold water). Add all of the other ingredients and blend together. This may be put into a mold or a square (7x11-inch) pan and chilled several hours or preferably overnight.

Fudge Pie

2 eggs beaten
½ cup melted margarine
1 cup sugar mixed with 4 T. cocoa
½ cup flour
pinch of salt
1 t. vanilla
½ cup nuts

Mix the ingredients as listed. Bake in a 400° oven for about 20 minutes, or until a good crust forms on the top and bottom. Serve hot with ice cream or whipped cream. The center should be "gooey."

Corn Sticks

If you have a pan that makes corn sticks, these look very attractive and will go nicely with the meal. However, this same recipe may be used for making corn muffins or corn bread. If you do not wish to make them from scratch, there are many convenient ready-to-use mixes that may be purchased.

1 cup milk
¼ t. baking soda
½ t. salt
1 t. baking powder
1 T. sugar
1 cup presifted flour
1 cup cornmeal
1 egg, lightly beaten

Preheat oven to 400°. Grease the corn stick or muffin pan. In a mixing bowl combine the milk, baking soda, salt, baking powder, and sugar. Stir until the sugar is dissolved. Add the flour and cornmeal. Stir until smooth. Add the egg and beat well. Spoon the batter into the pans or cups, filling them about ¾ full. Bake in a preheated oven for 20 to 25 minutes, or until lightly brown on the top.

*How convenient it is
to be a partial
Christian rather than
a whole-hearted one.*

Picnic on the Patio

Menu

(Serves 6 to 8)

Berry Punch

Raw Vegetables with Dip

Stuffed Hamburgers   **Hot Dogs on the Grill**

Macaroni Salad   **"Picnic" Beans**

Corn on the Cob—on the Grill

Buttermilk Coconut Pie   **Chocolate Chip Cake**

Sun Tea   **Lemonade**

Fresh Fruit

Summertime is a great time for entertaining! Almost any kind of food tastes good (or even better) when it is eaten outside. The out-of-doors has an amazing effect upon appetites (be sure to have plenty of food!), and the casualness of being outside gives an enjoyable, relaxed feeling to any get-together.

Your idea of a picnic may be on the patio, or at your favorite state park, or near the water. In our community we have a city park that is on a scenic lake. No homes have been allowed to be built on the land around the lake and it is an ideal setting for picnics anytime from May to October.

This is not your "typical" fried-chicken-potato-salad picnic, but you may add those traditional picnic items if you wish. Some of the recipes may become family favorites after enjoying them. So bring out the warm sunshine, set up your grill, and enjoy a picnic in the "good old summertime."

—Cindy

Berry Punch

**2 10-ounce packages frozen
raspberries, thawed**
1 cup bottled lime juice
**1 6-ounce can frozen orange juice,
thawed**
½ cup water
2 quarts ginger ale, chilled

*Mix the raspberries, lime juice, orange
juice, and water. Refrigerate. Pour the
chilled mixture over ice cubes in the
punch bowl. Stir in the ginger ale
gently. Garnish with orange slices and
mint sprigs.*

Raw Vegetables with Dip

*Choose your favorites and arrange
them on a platter with the dip. In
addition to the usual (but good)
carrots, celery, broccoli, and cauliflower, you may want to add zucchini,
cucumber, peppers, and radishes.*

Dip

1 pint (2 cups) mayonnaise)
**1 double package Hidden Valley
Ranch (original) dressing mix**
**1 16-ounce carton cottage cheese
(small curd and creamed)**

*Combine the listed ingredients and
refrigerate. This tastes better if it is
made the day before.*

Stuffed Hamburgers

6 to 8 servings.

2 T. butter or margarine
1¼ cups cornbread (or your
    favorite) stuffing
1 egg, beaten
1 4-ounce can chopped
    mushrooms, drained
⅓ cup beef broth
¼ cup sliced green onion
¼ cup chopped toasted almonds
1 t. lemon juice
3 pounds ground beef
1 t. salt

Melt butter in a saucepan over low heat; remove from heat. Add stuffing, egg, mushrooms, beef broth, green onion, almonds, and lemon juice; mix well and set aside. Combine ground beef with salt; shape into 16 patties.

Top 8 patties with stuffing mixture, using ¼ cup per patty. Cover with remaining patties; pinch edges together to seal. Place patties over medium coals and cook according to desired doneness.

Hot Dogs on the Grill

Choose your favorite brand, and just a short time before eating, put them on the grill. Watch them carefully because they cook very quickly. Serve with buns and your favorite condiments.

"Picnic" Beans

Serves 6 to 8.

1 10¾-ounce can tomato soup,
    undiluted
1 T. Worchestershire sauce
2 strips bacon, crumbled
6 T. chopped onion
½ cup chopped green pepper
1 T. prepared mustard
½ cup light molasses
2 16-ounce cans pork and beans

Combine all the ingredients except the pork and beans. Let stand 15 minutes. Add the pork and beans, mixing well. Spoon into a greased 2-quart shallow baking dish. Bake at 325° for 1½ hours.

Fresh Corn on the Cob

6 to 8 ears sweet corn
¼ cup soft butter or margarine

Remove silk from ears of corn; leave the husks on. Soak the corn in cold water for a few minutes; then tie the husks securely around the ears with long grass or string. Place on the coals and roast until the husks are nearly black. Remove from the coals; discard the husks and spread the ears with butter.

Macaroni Salad

1½ T. lemon juice
1 T. salad oil
2 cups cooked elbow macaroni
2 T. chopped chives
1 cup chopped celery
½ cup chopped stuffed olives
¾ t. salt
pepper to taste
2 T. chopped pimento
¼ cup sour cream

In a large mixing bowl beat the lemon juice and oil. Add the macaroni and toss lightly. Chill for 1 hour. Add all the remaining ingredients and again toss. Chill. Place in a serving dish at picnic time.

What a panorama of beauty our Creator puts forth to adorn the earth!

Chocolate Chip Cake

1 package yellow cake mix
1 small package chocolate or
    chocolate fudge instant pudding
    mix
1 small package vanilla instant
    pudding
½ cup oil
1½ cups water
4 eggs
1 t. vanilla
1 6-ounce package chocolate
    chips

Blend all the listed ingredients except the chocolate chips. After blending well, fold in the chocolate chips. Pour into a greased and floured bundt or tube pan. Bake at 325° for 1 hour. There is no need for a frosting, since this is a very moist and rich cake.

Sun Tea

1 gallon tap water
4 tea bags

Place the tea bags in the water in a gallon container with a lid. Place in the sun for several hours. When ready to serve, pour over ice.

Buttermilk Coconut Pie

5 eggs
1 stick margarine
1 cup buttermilk
2 cups sugar
1 cup coconut
1 9-inch unbaked pie shell

Mix the listed ingredients well and pour into the unbaked pie shell. Bake at 350° until done (about 30 minutes).

"God has called us to live in peace"
(1 Cor. 7:15).

Don't get discouraged;
God is still working with me.

Fresh Fruit

Pick your favorite summertime fruits and arrange them on a platter. They are the perfect ending to a picnic.

Saturday Night Supper

Menu

(Serves 6)

Beefy Vegetable Soup

Crusty French Bread

Cheese Souffle

Apple Salad

Fresh Orange Cake

When I was growing up, Saturday night was when I (and then my sister as she got older) became the cook. I'd plan the menu with my mom and then she'd buy the ingredients I'd need for Saturday night. The results weren't always pleasing to the appetite, but the experience was great and helped me develop my love for cooking.

The menu given here is for that special time when everyone is together and can enjoy a well-prepared dinner. It would be somewhat complicated for a "young cook" to make the entire meal, but there are several things that one can do or help with, so mom doesn't have to do it all.

Another suggeston for Saturday night could be a "do it yourself" pizza supper! Or let a family member take his or her turn picking out their favorite recipes and helping make some (or all) of the food.

—Cindy

Beefy Vegetable Soup

Makes 6 to 8 servings.

2½ pounds beef shank, cut into
   1-inch pieces
4 cups water
1 1 pound can tomatoes
1 medium chopped onion
1 T. salt
2 t. Worcestershire sauce
1 bay leaf
1 cup diced celery
1 cup sliced carrots
1 cup diced potatoes
1 cup chopped cabbage

Remove the meat from bone; cut into bite-size pieces; brown in hot fat. Put the bones, water, tomatoes, onions, and seasonings in a large kettle. Cover and simmer (meat included) 2 hours. Add the vegetables and simmer 1 hour longer. Remove bones and bay leaf before serving.

The vegetables called for in this soup are only suggestions. I always like to "clean out the refrigerator" and add all of our leftover vegetables. Sometimes I substitute barley instead of cabbage.

When you pray your deepest longings are understood and your hurts cushioned.

Apple Salad
Serves 6.

6 large eating apples (Jonathan, Red Delicious, Stayman are some of the varieties)
lemon juice
1½ cups diced celery
2 bananas, diced
1 cup coarsely chopped walnuts
mayonnaise
lettuce

Core apples, leaving bottoms whole. Hollow out, leaving a ½-ounce shell. Sprinkle cavities and apple pulp with lemon juice. Chop the pulp; add celery, banana, and nuts. Moisten with mayonnaise to taste. Mix well and fill apples, piling the mixture up in the center. Chill. Serve on lettuce.

There can be no rainbow without a cloud and a storm.

Crusty French Bread

Serves 8.

**1 loaf of your favorite French or
   sourdough bread
melted margarine or butter
garlic salt**

*Cut the loaf of bread in half,
lengthwise. Spread the margarine or
butter on the bread. Sprinkle with
garlic salt. Put the halves together
and wrap in foil. Place in the oven for
about 15 minutes at 400°. To serve,
slice crosswise.*

Cheese Souffle

Makes 6 servings.

**3 T. butter or margarine
3 T. flour
1 cup milk
⅓ cup grated Parmesan cheese
⅓ cup shredded Cheddar cheese
3 egg yolks, beaten
4 egg whites, stiffly beaten**

*Lightly butter a 1½ quart soufflé dish.
Melt butter or margarine in a saucepan; gradually add flour, stirring constantly until bubbly. Gradually add
milk; bring to a boil, stirring constantly.
Remove from heat. Add cheese; stir
until melted. Gradually stir in egg
yolks; cool. Fold egg whites into
cheese mixture. Spoon into soufflé
dish. Bake at 350° for 25 to 30
minutes. Serve immediately.*

*The best gift we can give at
Christmas is the one that costs
the most—ourselves.*

Fresh Orange Cake

½ cup shortening
1½ cups sugar
2 eggs
2¼ cups sifted flour
2 t. baking powder
¼ t. baking soda
½ cup orange juice
½ cup milk
1 t. grated orange peel

Preheat oven to 350°. Grease and flour two 9-inch layer cake pans. Into mixing bowl sift together flour, sugar, baking powder, and baking soda. Put orange juice into measuring cup and add milk to total 1 cup. Add with shortening and orange peel to flour mixture. Beat for 2 minutes on medium speed with electric beater. Add eggs; beat for 2 minutes longer. Pour into pans. Bake in preheated oven for 25 to 30 minutes. Cool for 10 minutes; remove from pans; cool on wire racks. Fill and frost with frosting.

Creamy Nut Filling and Frosting

2½ T. flour
½ cup milk
½ cup butter or margarine
½ cup sugar
½ cup chopped pecans
½ t. vanilla
1 cup powdered sugar (sift if lumpy)

Combine flour and milk in saucepan. Cook over medium heat, stirring constantly until thickened and smooth. Cool. Meanwhile, in a mixing bowl beat butter or margarine and sugar until light and fluffy. Add milk mixture; beat until fluffy and smooth. Stir in nuts and vanilla. Use ⅓ of mixture to fill the cake. Blend the powdered sugar into the remaining mixture and use to frost the sides and top of cake.

I love the stars too much to be afraid of the night.

Weekend Brunch

Menu

Fruit Pizza

Chicken Appetizers

Honey Dip

Sausage Corn Bread

Church Bread (Raisin Bread)

Potato Doughnuts

Coffee, Milk, Juice

Brunch, using the two words, *breakfast* and *lunch*, to make a new blend—brunch, has become an American favorite over the last few years. Brunch can be anytime, but with working schedules, the weekend seems to be the best time for this offering. Scrambled eggs, special breakfast meats, pancakes, French toast can all be offered at brunch, but this menu gives a little different variety and most of it can be made the night before.

These recipes may be used as a guide—I'm sure you will want to interject a few of your friends' or family's favorites. So pick the best day and time for you, and enjoy the American custom of brunch.

Fruit Pizza

1 package roll sugar cookie dough (found in the refrigerator section at the grocery)
1 8-ounce package cream cheese, softened
⅓ cup sugar
½ t. vanilla
Assorted fresh fruit*
½ cup orange marmalade or peach or apricot preserves
2 t. water

Slice the cookie dough ⅛-inch thick and line the pizza pan with the slices. Lightly press the pieces together, slightly overlapping. Bake at 375° for 10 to 12 minutes, or until lightly browned. Cool. Cream the sugar, cream cheese, and vanilla together. Smooth over the cooled cookie crust. Arrange any assortment of fruit beginning at the outer edge and working inward.

*Bananas, fresh strawberries, peaches, blueberries, grapes, pineapple, sliced apples may all be used. Choose three of your favorites and arrange them on the dough.

Mix the preserves (or marmalade) and water together. Pour this over the fresh fruit—use more if necessary. Chill. Cut into wedges when ready to serve.

Just as sunshine follows rain, we can believe that our prayers are heard and we are sustained.

Chicken Appetizers with Honey Dip

½ cup mayonnaise
1 t. dry mustard
1 t. minced onion
½ cup fine dry bread crumbs
¼ cup sesame seeds
2 cups cubed cooked chicken or
   turkey

Mix the first three ingredients together and set aside. Mix the crumbs and sesame seeds. Coat the chicken with the mayonnaise mixture and roll in the crumb mixture. Place on a baking sheet and bake for 12 minutes in a 425° oven, or until lightly browned. Serve hot with dip.

Where there is great love, there are always great miracles.

Honey Dip

Mix 1 cup mayonnaise with 1½ table-spoons honey.

Sausage Corn Bread

Makes 8 servings.

½ **pound hot or mildly seasoned
  sausage**
¼ **cup sausage grease or other
  shortening**
2 **cups self-rising cornmeal**
1 **t. sugar**
¼ **t. baking soda**
1 **egg, slightly beaten**
1½ **cups buttermilk**

Preheat oven to 450°. Fry the sausage until done and crumbly. Drain off the grease and add enough shortening to it to make ¼ cup. Put the shortening (or sausage grease) into a 9- or 10-inch black iron skillet. Place it in the hot oven. Combine the cornmeal, sugar, and soda. Add the egg to the buttermilk; stir into the dry ingredients. Remove the skillet carefully from the oven. Pour the hot shortening into the batter and stir very hard. Pour the batter (to which the sausage has been added) back into the hot skillet. Place in the oven and bake for 25 to 30 minutes, or until done and brown.

Church Bread (Raisin Bread)

I don't know where this bread got its name, but the recipe was given to me by a friend who has converted an old church into a beautiful home. It makes two large loaves and will freeze very well.

1 **pound box golden raisins**
2 **cups water**
1 **scant t. soda**
1 **cup cold water**
2 **cups sugar**
1 **t. salt**
1 **t. cinnamon**
½ **t. cloves**
1 **t. nutmeg**
4 **cups flour**

Boil the pound of raisins in 2 cups of water for 15 minutes. A large Dutch oven works well—all the ingredients can be mixed together, and there is only one pan to wash. Add the remaining ingredients and mix well. (It is not necessary to drain the raisins.) Pour into 2 greased and floured loaf pans (9x5x2¾ inches is the approximate size) and bake at 350° for about 50 to 55 minutes. Check the center carefully, as they may need to bake a little longer depending on the variation of your oven.

Potato Doughnuts

Makes about 3 dozen.

**1 cup sieved cooked potatoes
   (warm or cold)**
**1 cup liquid reserved from cooking
   potatoes**
¾ cup shortening
½ cup sugar
1 T. salt
1 package active dry yeast
¾ cup warm water (105° to 115°)
2 eggs, beaten
5 to 6 cups flour
oil
glaze

Mix the potatoes, potato liquid, shortening, sugar, and salt. Dissolve yeast in warm water; stir into potato mixture. Stir in eggs and enough flour to make dough easy to handle. Put the dough on a lightly floured surface; knead until smooth and elastic, 5 to 8 minutes. Place in a greased bowl; turn greased side up and cover with a clean tea towel. Let rise until double, 1 to 1½ hours. (Do not punch down.*) Pat the dough out on a lightly floured surface to ¾-inch thickness. Cut the doughnuts with a floured 2½-inch cutter. Let rise until double, about 1 hour. Heat the oil (3 to 4 inches) to 375° in a heavy pan. Fry the doughnuts until golden, 2 to 3 minutes on each side. Drain on a paper towel. Glaze doughnuts while warm.

*At this point the dough can be stored in the refrigerator 3 days before using. Refrigerate in a greased bowl immediately after kneading. Grease the top of the dough generously and cover with a damp towel. If dough rises in the refrigerator, punch down and cover with a damp towel.

Glaze

6 cups powdered sugar
1 cup boiling water

Mix the powdered sugar and boiling water until the consistency of gravy. Spread on warm doughnuts.

Store doughnuts at room temperature covered with a towel. They are best if they are eaten the same day they are fried.

1. Use the leftover liquid in pickle jars as a "marinade" for carrot and celery sticks. Very tasty!

2. For even, golden-brown baking remember this rule of thumb: Thick things (such as loaf cakes and bread) go in the bottom $\frac{1}{3}$ of the oven, and thin things (such as cookies) go in the top $\frac{1}{3}$.

3. To keep your tossed salads from getting soggy, place an inverted saucer in the bottom of the salad bowl. Then the extra liquid from dressings drains off under the saucer.

4. Try brushing downward on a corncob with a dampened tooth brush to remove all the cornsilk.

5. Keep fresh fruits from turning brown by tossing them with lemon juice. The juice of half a lemon is enough for 1 to 2 quarts of cut fruits.

6. Use kitchen scissors, rather than a knife, to cut marshmallows and dried fruits. Much easier!

7. If your gravy turns out too greasy, skim across the gravy with a paper towel or lettuce leaf. Either one will pick up excess grease.

8. Freeze leftover coffee or tea in ice cube trays. Then use the cubes to chill iced tea or iced coffee without diluting the beverage.

9. Add one teaspoon of vinegar to red cabbage near the end of its cooking time to preserve its red color.

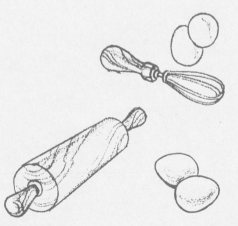